Bats

Most Unique Mammal!

Dr. Richard A. NeSmith

Love of Nature Series

ISSUE 29

Applied **P**rinciples of **E**ducation & Learning

APE-Learning *Publications*

© **2021 Richard A. NeSmith**
Love of Nature Series

dr.nesmith@gmail.com

https://bit.ly/3ZRFdDs

JUNE 2025

ISBN: 9798591526023

FLESCH-KINCAID GRADE LEVEL: 8.3

Bats
(order Chiroptera)

Bat is a Norwegian word meaning *leather flapper*, which

Native Americans related bats with *death* and *darkness*. This image of death and doom has been exaggerated and exploited by horror films linking bats to vampires and bloodsuckers. More recently, bats have been getting the blame for such causes as COVID-19, of which there is little real evidence.[1] On the other hand, Hollywood took the Dark Knight™ and made him a relatively positive crimefighter named Batman™, along with Batgirl™. Generally, fear is based on a lack of knowledge, and the fear of bats is no exception. The more one knows about bats, the less fearful one becomes.

Bats are not birds. Neither are bats rats, though they are often wrongly considered rodents. They are more closely related to **primates**.[2] Bats are mammals of the order **Chiroptera**, meaning *hand-wing*, and makeup nearly 25 percent of all mammal species. That's one in four mammals! A pretty significant number for a mammal we seldom see.

The bat's wings are literally their *hands*, *feet*, and *tail* covered

Little brown bat. (Myotis *lucifugus*)

---

[1] When one sees the frequent use of the word "probably" when determining the origin of this virus, this means it is more speculative than science.

[2] A 1982 study found that megabats share with primates a variety of complex details in the organization of neural pathways that have not been found in any other mammalian group, particularly not in microbats.

with a thin skin **membrane.** This skin stretched across the elongated arm and hand bones makes up 95% of its body surface area. The bat's hands are unusually stretched out far beyond that of most mammals, creating a vast **wingspan.**

They are, in fact, the *only* mammals able to fly.[3] And fly they do! Bats can *move with greater control* during flight than birds because of their ability to flap their wings independently (out of synch).[4]

Range

There are about 1,400 **species** of bats worldwide. Bats are found on every part of the planet except extreme deserts, a few isolated oceanic islands, and the polar regions.[5] There are 40 species of bats living in the United States and Canada, and possibly twice that number in Mexico. The state of New Mexico has reported 25 species of bats, while Arizona has 28. The majority of bats in the world inhabit tropical forests. That number in total easily outnumbers all the rest of the mammals combined.

Because bats are **mammals,** it seems useful here to

---

[3] The only nearest mammal to come close is the flying squirrel but they actually only glide.

[4] They are able to control wing shape (morphology) according to the aerodynamic demands more so than birds.

[5] Bats have been found near the Arctic Circle, but none in Antarctica.

understand what it means to be a mammal.

INTRODUCTION TO MAMMALS

Like humans, bats are mammals. Mammals have hair, give birth to live young, and feed their young on milk from the mother's mammary glands. Mammals number nearly 500

species on the continent of North America.[6] To better understand bats, we need to consider what a mammal is and its characteristics.

There are ***five traits that all mammals share in common***: These include that they are:

1. covered with hair or fur

2. warm-blooded

3. usually born alive and relatively well-developed

4. fed while very young with milk after birth produced by mammary glands

5. larger and more complex brains than any other group of animals

Hair has a vital function in mammals. It acts to insulate against the cold by conserving body heat. Specialized hairs

---

[6] Note: In the *Love of Nature* series we focus on North American species, however, in this issue we have also included some photographs of bats that are not from North America. There are several reasons for this but because these animals are so interesting and unique, we have decided to do so.

called **vibrissae**, or whiskers, serve as sensory organs for some nocturnal animals, including bats. The specially modified hairs on bats sense the speed and direction of air flowing over their wings.

All mammals are **warm-blooded** animals and breathe oxygen and release carbon dioxide. Being warm-blooded does not mean they prefer warm temperatures over the cold. It merely indicates that they create their own body

heat internally. *Warm-blooded* animals are **endothermic** (**endo-** *inside or internal*), meaning they make the needed body heat from food and energy breakdown (**metabolism**) generated by the liver. A mammal's **body temperature** is maintained at a *near-constant level* regardless of the external conditions. This, however, requires a great deal of energy and so more food.

Mammals also carry their unborn in the **uterus**[7] for more

extended periods than other animals, called **gestation**.[8] The time spent developing in the uterus varies in length from 13 days (as in the opossum) to 660 days (for elephants).[9] For bats, we will find pregnancy lasts much longer than that of other mammals their size. Newborn offspring are fed from their mother's **milk glands**. All mammals have some degree of maternal care.

---

[7] Uterus is the organ in a female mammal in which the young develop prior to birth.
[8] Gestation is the length of time a mammal develops and grows inside its mother's body before being born.
[9] See *Love of Nature series*, Issues: 13 (Opossums: Misunderstood Critter).

Mammals have the largest brains when comparing the body-to-brain ratio.[10] This expansion gives mammals an advantage and often enables mammals to have an incredibly developed *sense*, whether it be **smell** (as in bears) or **sight** (as in eagles), or in some bats, the ability to navigate by **echolocation**.

Characteristics

Bats come in all sizes. The world's smallest mammal in North America is a bat, the bumblebee bat.[11] This bat weighs less than a penny and has a wingspan of six inches (15 cm). The largest bat in the United States is the greater mastiff bat (Eumops *perotis*), with a two-foot (60 cm) wingspan.

Flight

---

[10] In an animal's history, most increased body size faster than brain size, with the exception of bats.
[11] Craseonycteris *thonglongyai*. Also called the hog-nosed bat.

One of the mega fruit bats.

Since bats are the only mammals that can fly, it seems useful to understand this means of transportation. Some bat species can fly distances up to 200 miles. During flight, a bat's heart rate can reach between 800 to nearly 1000 beats per minute. Bats have been spotted as high as 10,000 feet (3048 m) in the troposphere. Some bats have been observed hunting and stalking insects at 2624 feet (800 m) above ground level.

To fly, a bat has to drop from its perch.[12] If it is on the ground, it usually crawls to some height until it can fall into the air. Unlike birds, bats cannot launch their bodies into the air from the ground because their wings do not produce enough **lift** to take off. If fallen or knocked down

---

[12] Most bats cannot take flight from the ground. They must drop 2 or 3 feet before they can fly.

to the ground, the bat will appear ill. It is not sick; it merely has become immobile.

Why bats sleep upside down is still debated today. But it is evident that if sleeping bats need to be able to escape quickly. Hanging upside-down ensures they are already in the perfect position to spread their wings and fly away. And since their flexible wing cannot produce enough uplift to fly straight upward, they will fly in a circle cyclone pattern

Some bats cluster. One reason for this is to share body heat regulating the habitat temperature.

to create an updraft. Even during flight, a bat must *swoop down* to turn or regain speed.

Most animals could not hang upside down for long because the blood would begin to pool in the brain. Bats' bodies, however, are much smaller, and gravity does not have the same effect. Also, as they hang, their knees face backward, and they have special tendons that lock their toes in place. In other words, their feet automatically and mechanically "lock" in position onto whatever they are clinging to, caused just by the weight of their body. This structural difference allows them to hang freely while relaxed.

Landing upside down on a perch is not only a unique behavior but requires some unusual movement, too. Observations using high-speed cameras have shown that while flipping over, a bat pulls its wing in closer to its body while leaving the other one extended fully. The weight shift taking place creates **inertia** enabling them to land feet up in just a split second of time.

A bat's flight is much different than that of a bird. When a bat flies, it moves its wings like a human would use their hands when swimming. In other words, they "row" or paddle through the air. A bat's wings are like webbed hands. They can fold their wings, the way we can move or close our hands with our fingers. This characteristic provides them with a great deal more control of flight and

Photo is looking up in a cave into a crevice where bats have clustered.

the ability to maneuver in mid-air. Also, very strong back and chest muscles enable them to pull up (up-strokes) and down (down-strokes).

Upstrokes result from bats folding their wings. This move reduces the opposition (drag) from the air (air resistance)[13] and requires less energy. The down-stroke pushes their wings wide and downward with tremendous force, providing thrust and airlift, causing them to rise upwards.

These skills, often learned by observing their mother, enable them to dive through the air sharply, weaving in and out quickly as no bird can do. Many bats can hover in mid-air like a helicopter or a hummingbird. Some can glide for short periods and stop suddenly. Bats frequently fly low when hunting for insects. Some bats species can travel around 50 miles per night but return to their roosting tree, cave, or box.

---

[13] Drag and air resistance are synonymous. It is a type of friction or resistance; a force acting opposite to the relative motion of any object moving with respect to a surrounding air or fluid environment.

One cannot discuss the flight of bats without some understanding of **echolocation**.

Echolocation

Contrary to common belief, bats are not blind. They have eyes and can see, though not necessarily with the sharpness and colorful vision humans possess. They do have a large number of **rods**, which enhance *night vision*. Also, some bats

are also enhanced with the ability to see at night in two very different ways: **echolocation** and **ultraviolet light**.[14] This rare ability of echolocation in mammals was not discovered until 1940 and led to the development of technology we now call **radar** or **sonar**.[15]

Echolocation is a physiological process in which the bat

---

[14] This was discovered in a lab as recent evidence shown using genetics, use of immunology, histology, chemistry, and laboratory behavioral trials. The results indicated that many bats can see ultraviolet light (UV), at least at illumination levels similar to or brighter than those before twilight (down to a wavelength of 310 nm).

[15] Bats, dolphins, shrews , and some whales use echolocation. In addition, a few birds such as swiftlets (Australian and Asian bird) *and* oilbirds (South American bird) have been noted to have this ability, as well.

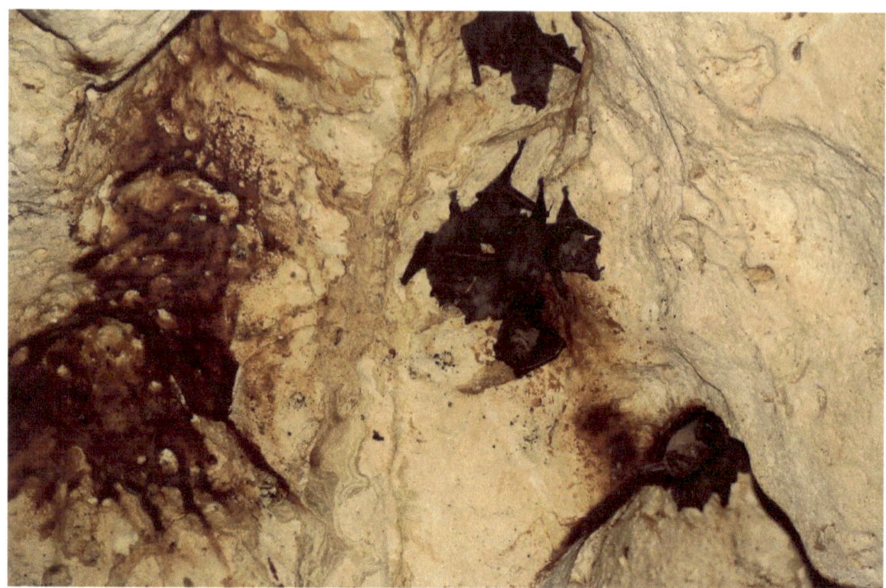

can produce **high-frequency** clicking sounds[16] (with their mouth, or more precisely, their larynx),[17] with various intensities and durations. Then, with their ear canals and flaps being angled, they hear the returned clicking sounds bouncing off objects within their environment[18]. These features allow them to **triangulate** their prey's exact location, including both a sense of the object's size, shape, texture, and how far the object is away (distance). And all of this is done in real time. That is truly amazing!

Echolocation involves both the **mouth** and **ear structures**. Covering the mouth has been demonstrated to restrict a bat from emitting these noises. Covering their ear with wax restricts their reception of these high-frequency sounds. In short, echolocation is a matter of bouncing sound ways off of objects enabling one to avoid a collision or to recognize

---

[16] Usually within the range of 20 to 200 kHz, which is beyond that of the human ear (12-20 kHz).

[17] It has been found that a few species of bats can produce the high-frequency sounds through their nose (via nasal passages).

[18] Some moths have been found to try to "jam" the bat's radar detection by creating clicking noises of their own.

prey and potential food. The benefits for those bats that have this sense are many, but it allows them to fly and navigate at night, even in total darkness.

There are several ways bats can be categorized. One way is by *relative size*, and another is by social *practices*.

Category by Size

Though bats come in various sizes, they can be characterized as larger or smaller. **Microbats,** found worldwide, are those bats on the smaller end of the size scale, whereas **macrobats** are larger and tend to be called *Old World* fruit bats. Microbats consist of the suborder **Microchiroptera** and possess **echolocation**.

Compared to Microchiroptera, megabats (**Megachiroptera**) are much larger and live in tropical and subtropical climates. The most significant difference is that most megabats do not have echolocation abilities, nor do they eat insects. Most eat fruit, nectar, or pollen (nectarivorous and frugivorous diets) and are very important in pollinating

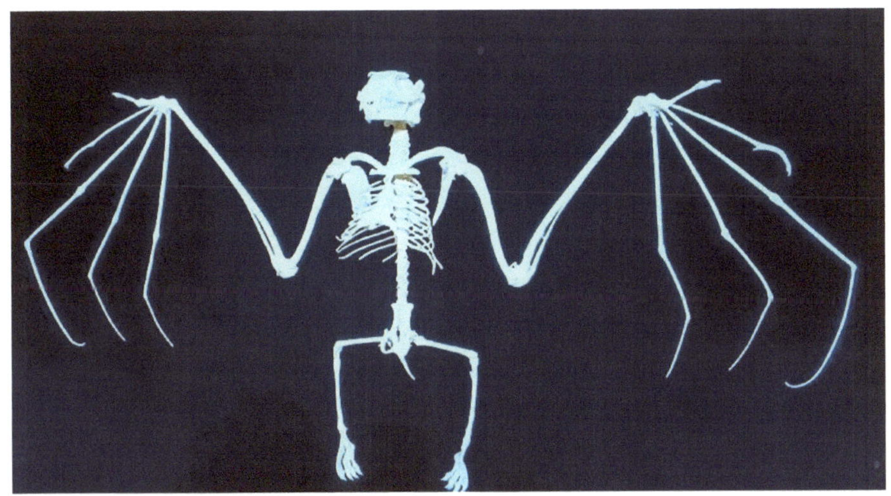

plants, such as the saguaro cacti in southern Arizona.[19]

Bat behavior makes bats extremely valuable to farmers and agriculture. This is true not just for their importance in pollination but in controlling pests that target crops or livestock.[20] In some areas, bats consume enough insects to encourage farmers to use less pesticide on their crops.

Other differences include microbats lacking the claw at the forelimb's second finger but *possessing a **tail*** that megabats do not have, with a few rare exceptions. The ears of microbats contain a **tragus**, a piece of skin in front of the *ear canal*. This skin flap directs sounds into the ear for prey location and navigation. It is also an important feature in identifying bat species.

---

[19] Further south, the agave plant is pollinated by bats, which is the plant from which Tequila is made..

[20] One bat biologist (called a chiropterologist) estimated that in the United States bats save farmers $23 billion dollars every summer.

The eyes of the megabats are relatively larger. They have keener eyesight than those of the microbats, who supplement with echolocation. Finally, megabats also make their homes in trees, shrubs, and sometimes caves near water edges.

Bats play an integral role in the surrounding ecosystem because they help spread **seeds** and **pollen** by feeding

and feces.[21] Bats' feces is called **guano**. Bats can and do defecate and urinate while in flight. More will be said on this topic, but here we want to point out that fecal droppings and drops of urine may become splattered on

---

[21] It is estimated that 96% of the regrowth in the rainforests is due to seed dispersal from bats.

One of the microbats, of which most use echolocation and eat insects.

the outer and inner walls of a cave, trees, or buildings near where the bats gain entry or exit.

Category by Social Practice

Another manner of grouping bats is that they are either **colonial** or **solitary**. Colonial bats congregate in caves, mines, under bridges, and sometimes inside buildings. Solitary bats live primarily in trees but may enter buildings during spring and autumn migration. Bats will roost in buildings if their natural habitats are no longer available.

One of the more recent interventions helping bats survive includes building and placing **bat houses** or **bat boxes**. Installing a bat house on one's property provides a safe environment for bats. It also protects one's yard from pesty insects, including mosquitoes, moths, and beetles. As bats tend to huddle, bat houses also provide females with a safe, warm place to raise their young. Since most female bats only have one offspring (**pup**) each year, bat populations grow very slowly. Most bat **colonies** are presently in decline.

Hibernation

Winter poses two threats to bats: cold and starvation. Some bats, especially those living in cold, moderate climates, do hibernate or migrate to warmer areas. Some bat species hibernate, some migrate, and some do *both*. Hibernation periods can be very short or several months, depending on the species. Hibernation is mutually linked with temperature and food availability, which triggers hormonal mechanisms.[22] And in temperate climates, like Florida, bats may be able to stay year-round.

Homes are generally made in caves, mines, or other structures. *Tree bats*, however, do not require caves for hibernation. Instead, many species retreat to places such as tree cavities, cliff faces, or woodpiles. Their body, metabolism, and heart slow to a minimum to conserve

---

[22] The lipostat hormone leptin is strongly associated with winter energy balance and pre-hibernation fattening.

energy. This preserves their stored fat reserves. During hibernation times, they are especially susceptible to disturbances interrupting their "sleep" during this time. If they are aroused from hibernation, they can consume these fat reserves and lose the equivalent of 10 to 30 days' energy supply. This is more than just a disturbance during hibernation as it can cost bats their lives.

Even upon arousal, a bat may be incapable of flight for several minutes as it regains normal body functions. If knocked to the ground, it becomes immobile and appears to be sick. Often fallen bats are mistaken to be ill, sick, or rabid.

Those bats that hibernate do *genuinely* hibernate. It is not just a period of inactivity. It involves extreme physiological reductions in **metabolic rate**, heart rate, and respiratory rate, which allows a bat to survive prolonged periods without food. A bat's heart rate drops from 200-300 beats per minute to 10 beats per minute! Its breathing rate can be reduced to several minutes *per breath*. Bodily functions slow down, reducing energy costs by about 98%. A bat's body temperature can also drop to near freezing, depending on its surrounding temperature.

Bats require specific temperatures for hibernation ranging

from 35-40 degrees Fahrenheit (1.7-4.5°C). Big Brown bats, for example, have determined that attics provide a more beneficial temperature for survival during hibernation than caves. In this state of **torpor**, bats are highly efficient in energy saving. Still, they need to not wake due to any disturbance.

While their bodies function at a much lower energy consumption level, they are inactive and go into a deep sleep. **Torpor** permits them to conserve energy and survive the winter. Inactivity can be for just a few hours, several days at a time, or up to a month during cold winters. There are brief periods of awakening when the body temperatures return to normal for a few hours.

In the Northern United States and Canada, the little brown bat can hibernate for up to six months before feeding again in spring. This is why the bats' location and dwelling places are vitally important, particularly the ideal temperature and humidity. Some bats wrap themselves up with their wings

and long-furry tail membrane during the cold season to reduce heat loss to manage an ultimate temperature level. Such hibernation places are referred to as **hibernacula**.

Some bat species hibernate in dense **clusters** with other bats. Some roost alone. Clustering may help lessen dehydration and temperature fluctuation. However, clustering also brings more attention to bats or known bat hibernacula, making them extremely vulnerable to human disturbance and vandalism. Some known bat caves now have reinforced grates placed across them to keep people out during hibernation seasons.

Migration

Not all bats hibernate. And, not all bats spend their winter in caves. Some bat species like the spotted bat survive by

migrating in search of food to warmer areas when the weather gets chilly. Many North American bat species begin migrating to their chosen hibernation sites as early as September.

In North America, free-tailed bats migrate in considerable numbers to hibernation sites in Texas and Mexico. Compared with birds, bats migrate relatively short-distances. Even bats living in temperate regions seem to have broad migratory behaviors, from short migraters to mid-distance ones. Finally, some bats migrate 62-310 miles (100-500 km) between summer and winter roosts, and these are considered very long migrations for bats. Intercontinental migration is also relatively uncommon in bats.

Diet

Most bat species in North America are **insectivores**.[23] Bats are thought to catch and eat up 600 to 1,000 mosquito-

---

[23] At least 40 different kinds of bats in the U.S. eat nothing but insects. Worldwide, 70% of bats consume insects and small bugs for food. The other 30% consume various types of fruit.

sized insects in an hour's time.[24] A nursing mother bat can easily catch more than 4,000 insects in a night. However, they may also supplement their diets with a wide variety of food, including fish, frogs, lizards, rodents, birds, other bat species, and even blood.

Most bats eat flowers, small insects, fruits, nectar,[25] pollen, and leaves, though it depends on the species. Megabats usually eat fruit, and microbats generally eat insects. Some bats can eat as much as half their body weight every day in insects. Can you imagine eating half of your body weight,

---

[24] It was never stated that they feed like this amount ALL night, no more than if you sat down and ate 50 French fries in a given hour's time. In addition, some have reported this to be the number of mosquitos that could be eatin. It should be noted, however, that research studies have shown that mosquitoes make up less than one percent of the overall diet bat's diets. There is a reason for this. experts have found that the bats, especially larger ones, prefer larger insects like beetles, moths, or caddisflies that provide more calories per bug. Therefore, while there is some evidence that bats can help keep mosquitoes in check, claims that bats eat thousands of mosquitoes every night seem to be largely overstated.

[25] Only three southwestern species of bat feed on nectar.

say, in pizza or hamburgers, every day?

Nonetheless, approximately 70 percent of bats are the most significant predators of night-flying insects. There are at least 40 different kinds of bats in the U.S. that eat nothing but insects. A single little brown bat, which has a body no larger than an adult human thumb, can eat 0.14-0.28 ounces (4 to 8 grams). This is about the weight of one or

two grapes of insects per night.

Bat sometime get caught on barbed-wire fences and are unable to free themselves.

Once a bat has located an insect using its echolocation, it traps it with its wing or tail membranes and then moves the insect to its mouth. This movement can cause a somewhat awkward or erratic flight in the air, which most people easily notice while observing feeding bats. Most bats feed during the late evening or near lighted areas at night (since these locations attract many insects).

Behaviors

Because they are **nocturnal**, bats hunt at night and roost during the day in trees, bat boxes, under eaves, and inside of buildings where they can gain access through open spaces in roofs, attics, or walls. Bats may hide in crevices and other dark areas as well. They will typically stay close to bodies of water. Most active in the spring and summer, many bats migrate or hibernate during the winter.

When fruit-eating bats roost during the day, they do so high up in the trees. This behavior provides them with darkness and protects them from various predators. Bats tend to have few natural predators.

The National Institute of Health identified the leading causes of bat deaths. These included:

❶ **intentional killing by humans;**

❷ **predation, biotoxins;**

❸ **natural non-living (abiotic) factors** (e.g., weather, floods, fire, volcanism);

❹ **exposure to environmental contaminants, including pesticides;**

❺ **accidents** (e.g., entrapment, impalement, collisions with objects other than wind turbines);

❻ **collisions with wind turbines;**

❼ **infectious viral and bacterial diseases;**

❽ **the fungal disease white-nose syndrome** (WNS)

More bats die from **human *aggression*** than any other cause. One poll provided insight into the reasons people kill bats.[26] Some of the reasons given included: bats are evil if a bat flies over your head and pees on your face, you could go blind, they stink, they are loud, they're witches, if

---

[26] Merlin Tuttle's Bat Conseration. See: https://youtu.be/kW--eOLOrq0

one gets in your house that means something terrible is going to happen to the owner, bad luck or bad omen, they can slap you, afraid of getting diseases from them. People kill bats because of irrational fears, not because of validated facts. *People will not protect what they fear.* The answer to this problem is education; it is incredibly powerful in helping people understand the *benefits* of taking care of nature.

Also, bats are dying from electrocution on power lines, being caught on **barbed wire** fences, starved by deforestation, disturbed by light pollution, and paralyzed by ticks. Other bats die due to climate heatwaves, automobiles, and energy-producing wind generators. It is estimated that 10,000 to hundreds of thousands die being hacked up flying into wind turbines each year in North America alone. However, bats also have other *natural predators,* including owls, hawks, and snakes.

The biggest disease threat to bats mentioned above includes the **White-Nose Syndrome**.[27] This illness kills millions of bats each year. It is caused by a white *fungal infection* that spreads very rapidly from the northeastern shores to the central United States and infects the skin, mouth, ears, and wings of hibernating bats. This fungus basically starves them to death by increasing their energy consumption during winter hibernation, wasting stored fat.

Though **gas exchange** through the skin is uncommon in mammals, it occurs in bats. The skin of bats, however, is much thinner than most mammals. The back (dorsal) skin of bats has a standard thickness.[28] In most of a bat's body, the top thin tissue forms the outer layer of a body's surface (called the **epithelial**). The bat's surface skin consists of one to three cell layers, allowing for efficient gas exchange. Although one layer is relatively thick, oxygen (O_2) readily diffuses through the membrane, facilitating exchange with carbon dioxide (CO_2) as it moves between the environment and the underlying vessels.

The veins and blood vessels in a bat also help regulate

---

27 Pseudogymnoascus *destructans*. To date, there have been no reported human illnesses attributable to WNS.
28 About 605 μm

blood pressure, water balance, body temperature, and gas exchange. To increase or enhance **heat exchange**, some bats will **urinate** on their wings.

The behavior of *urinating on the wings* could explain why it is not uncommon for bats to emit a strong odor. Most of the scent, for example, from a large bat **colony**[29] is not produced by the bat feces or poop (**guano**) but by the bats themselves and their **urine**. As such, it has a musty, ammonia-type smell, and the larger the **colony**, the more pervasive and more decadent the smell becomes.

Since we are back on bats' bathroom habits, **guano** is a very rich fertilizer.[30] It can be used as a soil conditioner, enriching the soil and improving drainage and texture. Bat guano is a suitable fertilizer for plants and lawns, making them healthy and green. Guano can also be used as a natural fungicide and controls various worms (**nematodes**) in the soil.

[29] The largest colony on the planet is reported to be a 20 million bats materrnity colony in a single cave in San Antonio, Texas, called Bracken Cave.

[30] Also, as the guano decomposes it produces enough heat to moderate and raise the temperature within a cave environment, which can be particularly beneficial for winter or during the raising of bat pups.

Reproduction

By size, bats have a more *extended* gestation period than other mammals their own size. The majority of North American bats tend to mate in the autumn or winter before going into hibernation. The mating ritual often occurs at night since bats usually sleep in the daytime. The male bat awakens the female by biting her on the neck and then initiating **copulation**. If copulation occurs during the day, the male will begin sex by rubbing its head against the female.

Mating takes place upside down for some species, whereas other species mate on cave walls or rock crevices. The male bat takes hold of the female from behind. This encounter can be brief or long and noisy.

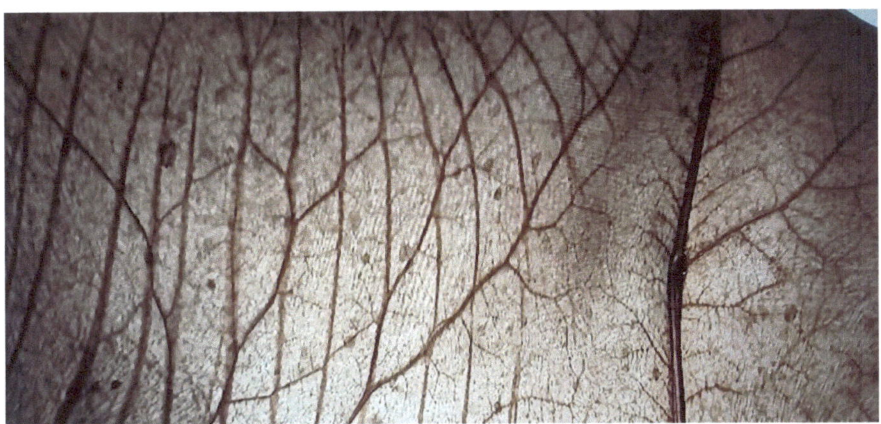

Close examination of the very thin skin making up the wings, reveals numerous blood vessels.

Most species of bats are unrestrained and will mate with multiple partners. In some cases, one or two males will acquire and defend a small harem of females. A few species are even **monogamous**, and the entire family will roost in a group once the pups are born.

After mating, the female stores the sperm (**spermatozoa**) until spring, waiting for her **ovulation cycle** (the release of an egg from her ovary into the **fallopian tube**).[31] The fertilized egg begins the long **gestation** period, which is considered a very long and slow process for mammals of the same size (from six to twenty-five weeks, depending on species).[32]

Pups are born upside down in the colony in late spring to early fall (species-specific) in time for adequate food accessibility. Most bats give birth to one or two pups, and in some species, up to six. Bat pups are born helpless, hairless, tiny, skinny, pink, and equipped with *milk teeth*.

Like other mammals, mother bats hold their babies close, carefully nurture and feed them breastmilk. The young one

---

[31] The male's sperm remains dormant but viable in the female's reproductive system until spring.
[32] Bats are considered one of the slowest reproducing animals in the world.

Special tendons in the legs work to automatically hold the bat in place will resting, preventing a bat from falling while sleeping.

stays latched on to its mother's body. Each mother bat can identify her own pup due to individualized clicking noises the offspring make. Nursing the pups will last about four to five weeks.

It is not uncommon for many bat pups to be weaned before their birth month ends as the mother bat nudges and prods her young to **fledge** (developed enough to fly). By the end of week three, many pups can be found on the ground as they learn to fly. Once flight is achieved, the pups begin to venture out from the roost to forage for food.

Depending on the species, the adolescent offspring tend to stay and learn various survival tactics from their mother and may even take turns hunting for food at night. This period is a crucial training period. It has been found that bats born in captivity cannot survive the wild not having this training.

Although most bats live less than 20 years in the wild, scientists have documented six species that live more than

Lake Meadnra California Leaf Bat

30 years. In 2006, a tiny bat from Siberia set the world record at 41 years.

Common Types of North American Bats

Of the 40 species of bats in North America, all of them are important. They serve a specific purpose and niche in their environments. Many bat species are considered **keystone species.** An animal that is a keystone species makes such a contribution to its habitat that removing it would change the environment and significantly affect the other animals in that habitat.

If bats were removed from their ecosystem, many animals and plants would be affected. Migratory species, in particular, influence two habitats. Here, we have selected 12 species for brief mention to help us become more familiar with these unique mammals. There are various species found in the United States. Some include:

Bat houses have become very important homes for bats as habitats are shrinking in some regions.

- Greater Mastiff (Eumops *perotis*)

- Little Brown Bat

- Bumble Bee Bat (Craseonycteris *thonglongyai*) (Kitti's Hog-nosed bat).

- Lesser long-nosed bat

- Vampire bats*

- Hoary bat

- Pallid bat

- Mexican free-tailed bat

- Virginia Big-eared Bat

- California Leaf-nosed Bat

- Mariana Fruit Bat*

- Indiana Bat*

*While most of the species mentioned are found in the United

States, the Bumblebee Bat, Mariana Fruit Bat, and Vampire Bat are notable exceptions.

Miscellaneous

Neither microbats nor macrobats attack humans. Not even vampire bats target humans.[33] Bats are, by nature, gentle animals. However, they are wild animals, and trying to pick one up or swoosh one out of the way can lead to them becoming defensive and can cause bites or scratches.

If a bat is found in your home, close the doors and open a screenless window. If you cannot do that, place a plastic bowl over it and slide cardboard behind it. Or, if  no other choice, throw a towel over it. Both practices can enable you to remove the bat from your home.

Very few bats contract **rabies**. ***Over the last 50 years***, fewer than 40 people have contracted rabies from a wild bat. That is one per year on average. In the decade between 2009-2018, 25 cases of human rabies have been reported in the United States, but bats were not the predominant

---

[33] Nor do they suck blood. Of the three species of vampire bats in North America, only a single specimen has been recorded for the United States in extreme southwest Texas. Vampire bats do not suck blood. Rather, they make a small incision with their sharp front teeth on another mammal and lap up the blood with their tongue. Vampire bats need to drink about one ounce of blood at every meal, meaning they consume half their body weight during each 20 to 30 minute feeding session.

carriers. Since 1990, only one human rabies case has been

verified to have occurred involving a bat in the United States.[34] According to the Centers for Disease Control (CDC), in the United States, the most common wild reservoirs of rabies are raccoons, skunks, bats, and foxes, followed by domesticated dogs and cats.[35]

These mammals are currently *under threat*. Though these five somewhat widespread pressures closely reflect the same factors that cause death, these are worth reviewing.

❶ hunting or annihilation   ❹ invasive species

❷ widespread habitat destruction   ❺ other stresses

❸ accelerated climate change

Bats are legally protected in North America. There are even current laws protecting bats when they occupy a home or building.[36] However, several concerned species have conservation issues, such as little brown bats and Florida bonneted bats, often found living in human-made structures.

These mammals are currently under threat as never before.

---

[34] Bats can carry rabies, but a person cannot become infected with rabies from having contact with bat guano (feces), blood, or urine or from touching a bat on its fur. The transmission must occur by being biten. In addition, a bat must be *sick with the disease* to pass it to another animal via a bite. Less than 1/10 of 1 percent (0.001); one out of 1000 chances, of a wild bat having rabies.

[35] See http://bit.ly/38fnNWW

[36] Anyone who knowingly harms a protected species is in violation of the ESA and can result in fines up to $50,000 and imprisonment for up to one year.

Six bat species in North America are considered **endangered species**. The Indiana bats, for example, are among the United States' most endangered bats. Action is needed, and if we do not act, plan, and execute, then once the decline begins, it will be almost impossible to stop. Bats, like no other mammal, are so very unique.

The Bat Conservation International stated it quite prophetically: "A world without bats would look very different than the one you know — and not for the better.''[37] **Bats: *Most unique mammal.***

REVIEW

1. What taxonomic order are bats in, and why does this word fit them so well?

2. How many different species of bats are found in North America?

3. What are the two main types of bats, and what similarities and differences do they have?

4. What two ways do bats live through cold winters?

5. How are microbats able to catch insects in the pitch black of night?

6. Explain what *echolocation* is and what is required to be able to use this system.

7. Explain how bats are so much better at maneuvering in flight than most birds.

8. Why would fruit-eating bats not need or use echolocation?

9. Why do some bats cluster together in caves or bat houses?

10. What are three things you found most fascinating about bats?

MEGABAT

COLORING PAGE

http://www.supercoloring.com/coloring-pages/bat

Name:_______________________

Bats: Most Unique Mammal!

Carefully read each statement or clue. Fill in the blanks provided in the proper boxes. Use the Word Bank if necessary.

tragus   pollination   metabolic   white   colony   blooded   hawks   hibernation   nocturnal

aggression   guano   insectivores   hibernacula   microchiroptera   frugivorous   migration

urinate

Across

1. Often done in response to cold weather or reduction in food availability.
2. Bats hunt at night because they are known to be __________.
5. Two major benefits of bats include spreading seeds and __________.
9. Classification of small bats that tend to eat insects.
11. Name for animals that eat only fruit.
13. Helps to direct sound into the ear canal.
14. Body metabolism slows as does the organs.
15. Bats gather and live together.

Down

1. __________ rate involves breaking down food to nutrients and energy.
3. Fungus causing lots of bat deaths is the __________-nose syndrome.
4. An animal that produces its own body heat is said to be warm-__________.
6. Name for animals that eat only insects.
7. Doodle-doodle-doodle, doo!
8. groups of bats hibernating together in clusters.
10. The main cause of bat deaths is from human __________.
12. Something some bats do on their wings to stay cool during hot days.
14. A natural predator of bats.

INTERESTING SOURCES TO CONSIDER

Understanding America's Big Cat: An Introduction to the Teton Cougar Project. National Geographic. Available at: https://blog.nationalgeographic.org/2013/11/27/understanding-americas-big-cat-an-introduction-to-the-teton-cougar-project/

https://www.doi.gov/blog/13-facts-about-bats

20 Most Bizarre Bat Species. Available at: https://youtu.be/gYJHcwwMo0E

All About Bats for Kids: Animal Videos for Children. FreeSchool. Available at: https://youtu.be/9FVoTMOorXA

All About Bats. Available at: https://www.nps.gov/subjects/bats/all-about-bats.htm

Bats! National Geographic. Available at: https://www.nationalgeographic.com/animals/mammals/group/bats/

Bats: The True Story. Available at: https://youtu.be/KcJZJtKmfLI

Conservation Connect Series: Bats. Available at: https://youtu.be/jiburwYOQXQ

Fun Facts About Bats. Available at: https://youtu.be/b3w9ZbRQIek

Journeying with Bats Across Mexico. Perpetual Planet: Mexico. Available at: https://youtu.be/87rzxT9p2gs

Killer Bats Of The Amazon (Wildlife Documentary). Austin Stevens Adventures. Available at: https://youtu.be/m-ujJOsroog

Season of the Bat. Available at: https://youtu.be/5nWxeuCMUO4

Secrets and Mysteries of Bats: Nature Documentary. Available at: https://youtu.be/vCbZHvsX1dk

Smallest Bat in the World! The Conservation Files (Ep. 6: AnimalBytesTV). Available at: https://youtu.be/GysHLFIvR1M

The Truth About Bats. Merlin Tuttle Bat Conservation. Available at: https://youtu.be/kW--eOLOrq0

Visiting the Largest Bat Colony on Earth!. Available at: https://youtu.be/P_tykwBvqZ0

ABOUT THE AUTHOR

Richard NeSmith is a native of Florida, USA. He grew up wading through the swamps of central Florida with his two younger brothers during the pre-Disney era, and unknowingly, falling in love with biology, wildlife, and nature. He has lived in seven American states, twice in Australia and once in Mexico City. He holds eight university degrees and has taught for 14 years in secondary schools, here and abroad, and another 13 years as a professor in several American universities. His service includes professor of science education, Dean of Education, Campus Dean, as well as an online instructor. His passion for learning (and *how we learn*) did not develop until *after* graduating from high school. His only explanation for this is that *having a goal made all the difference in the world*. He enjoys reading, hiking, nature photography, golf, tennis, and R.V. camping.

http://richardnesmith.obior.cc

Applied **P**rinciples of **E**ducation & Learning *presents*

APE-Learning

AMAZON AUTHOR's PAGE:

https://www.amazon.com/author/richardnesmith

Educational, wildlife, and naturalist books
Dr. Richard NeSmith.

Issue 1
Raccoons:
Friendly Bandits
Dr. Richard NeSmith

Issue 2
Sandhill Cranes
&
Pileated Woodpeckers
Flaming Redheads
Dr. Richard NeSmith

Issue 3
American
Alligators
&
Crocodiles
Dr. Richard NeSmith

Issue 4
Bobcats:
Ghostly Elusive
Dr. Richard NeSmith

Issue 5
Foxes:
Sneaky Rascals
Dr. Richard NeSmith

Issue 6
Armadillo:
Little Armored One
Dr. Richard NeSmith

Issue 7
Squirrels:
Bushy Tail Scampers
Dr. Richard NeSmith

Issue 8
River Otters:
Aquatic Clowns!
Dr. Richard NeSmith

Issue 9
Beavers:
Nature's Engineers!
Dr. Richard NeSmith

Issue 10
Black Bears
Titans of the Forest
Dr. Richard NeSmith

Issue 11
Freshwater
Turtles
Dr. Richard NeSmith

Issue 12
FUNGI, LICHENS
& MUSHROOMS
Dr. Richard NeSmith

Paperbacks: http://amazon.com/author/richardnesmith

e-books: https://bit.ly/3iuCgB3

---

[i] **Special thanks to the following who kindly provided permission to use their photographs.**

From Unsplash: David Clode, Dan Myers, Jackie Chin, Todd Cravens, Tommy Pequinot, Zdenek Machacek, Vishu Vishuma, and James Wainscoat.

From Pixabay: Shell Brown, alobenda, Bernell MacDonald, Signe Allerslev, Cindy Parks, Julie Duchesneau, Pexels, Walter Navarro, Mario Classico, seagull, MICHOFF, Dorothée Quennesson, Angeles Balaguer, Andre Zan, analogicus, Stephen Chantzis, Esmoth, Deedster, falco, and Botros Travel Solutions.

Finally, *special thanks* to likeminded friends who love wildlife and who willingly shared their wonderful photos, and many of whom have become my friends: **Peter Lyle**, **Amanda Harden**, **Jose Rodriguez**, **Tracey Burke Singletary**, *and* **Dr. Dan Rieck**.

http://www.joserodriguezphoto.com

If you enjoyed this book, please go to amazon.com and share a nice review. 

Thank you everyone.

Love Learning – Love Nature – Love Life